Arwen The Dreamer
The Greatest Present Ever!

By Arwen Di Blasio & Marge Di Blasio

Copyright © 2020 Marge Di Blasio

All rights reserved.

No part of this publication may be reproduced, distributed or transmitted in any form or by any means, including photocopying, recording, or other electronic or mechanic methods, without the prior written permission of the publisher, except in the case of brief quotations embodied in critical reviews and certain other non-commercial uses permitted by copyright law.

ISBN: 978-1-7774177-3-4 (Paperback) | ISBN: 978-1-7774177-1-0 (Hardcover)

Illustrated By Ayan Mansoori | Formatted By Ell Om

www.margediblasio.com

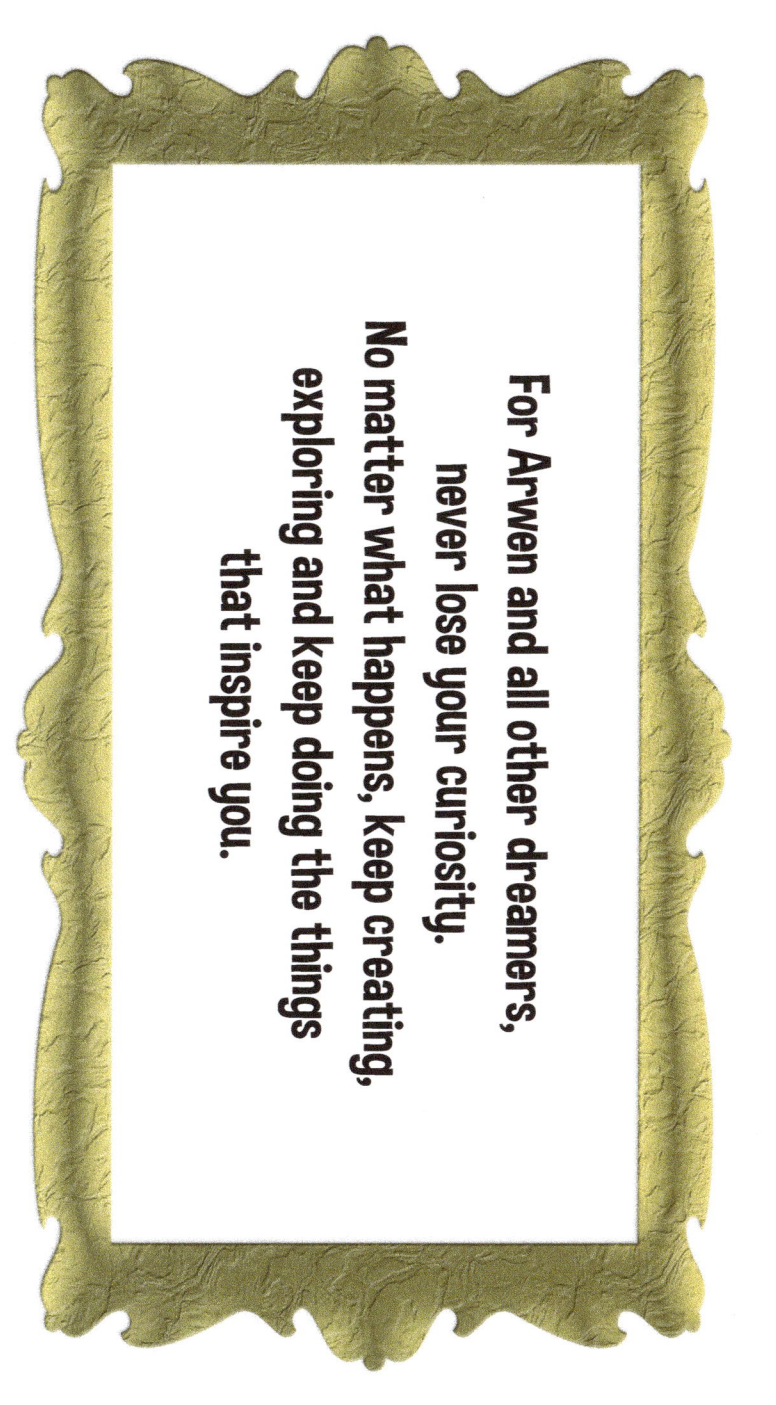

For Arwen and all other dreamers, never lose your curiosity. No matter what happens, keep creating, exploring and keep doing the things that inspire you.

It was a sunny day and all the other kids were playing outside, but Arwen didn't care. All she could think of was to prepare for the big day. Christmas was coming!

Arwen was overwhelmed with all the options she had.

Which one should I pick? Which one? I want to explore, play and have fun. Can I get them all? Why do I need to pick just one?

She walked toward her room. Inside her closet, she found her Christmas wish list.

"If I don't know what to do, should I just do eeny, meeny, miny, moe?" Arwen pondered.

"But I really want them all, so what will I do?"

Suddenly, she remembered what her Mom said, "If you can't decide now, take a break. Go for a walk, do something else. All you need to do is to sleep on it first."

And that's what Arwen did. She went to her room and whispered, "I'll take a nap. I'm sure to have a better idea when I wake up."

In her dream she imagined a frozen castle, lego bricks, melting beads, toys everywhere.

Then Arwen noticed the unusual silence in the room. She screamed, "Mom! Dad! Where are you?"

She even called out for her younger sister, Amelia, who loves to be around her, "Ameliaaaaa, Ameliaaaaa, where are you? Hmmm...where is everybody?"

She looked all over the house, but they were nowhere to be found. So she sat by the Christmas tree, surrounded by all the presents. The joy she had when she opened each gift started to fade away.

Suddenly she heard a little voice.

"Psst...psst...Arwen!" the little voice whispered.

She looked around and couldn't see anybody.

"Psst...Hello!" the little voice said.

As Arwen unwrapped the talking present, she saw a picture of her family together with a stone painted with the word "Love".

Why don't you open me up?

Arwen screamed, "What?!"
Suddenly tears fell from her eyes.

"No! I want my Mom, Dad, Amelia, my family! Please give them back to me now!"

Arwen realized that she could have all the toys she wanted, but it only gave her temporary happiness. Without her family, without love, she would never be complete.

The dream of getting all the presents wasn't enough to replace those she truly loved.

I want my Mom, Dad and sister! All these toys are only fun for a moment.

On Christmas Day...

Arwen realized that the greatest presents are usually the ones that we already have. The people around us. The greatest present she could ever receive is to love and be loved.

How about you?
What's the gift you want to receive this Christmas?

*Love is patient, love is kind.
It does not envy, it does not boast,
it is not proud.
It is not rude, it is not self-seeking,
it is not easily angered, and it keeps
no record of wrongs.
Love does not delight in evil
but rejoices with the truth.*

1 Corinthians 13, 4-6

*Love never ends...
And now these three remain:
faith, hope, and love.
But the greatest of these is love.*

1 Corinthians 13:13

One More Thing...

Thanks again for reading my first book.
I would love to hear what you think.

Could you please take a moment to review?

Your feedback can help others to learn more
about my book. It would also help
me understand how I can do better
and come up with more creative ideas
to share with you and others.

Many thanks,

Arwen Di Blasio

About the Authors

ARWEN DI BLASIO is a young creator who dreams of sharing her stories with the world. She loves drawing, painting, reading, creating different things and most of all, to have fun. Inspired by the books her mom has published, she wrote this book and collaborated with the illustrations when she was five years old.

MARGE CASTILLON DI BLASIO is an author, coach, wife, mother, daughter, sister, friend, and a lifelong learner. She wrote this book to cultivate creativity together with her daughter Arwen. When not working or writing, she disconnects from all the technology and focuses on the moment. Most of her spare time is spent with her loving husband and two beautiful daughters, family and friends.

Connect with Marge and Arwen!

www.margediblasio.com